DEVIN BOOKER

NBA STAR

By Douglas Lynne

Book design by Christine Ha
Cover design by Jake Norby

Photographs ©: Rick Scuteri/AP Images, cover, 1, 20; Elise Amendola/AP Images, 4, 7, 8, 23; Jack Smith/AP Images, 10; James Crisp/AP Images, 13; Tim Gangloff/Cal Sport Media/AP Images, 14; Matt York/AP Images, 16; Chris Pizzello/AP Images, 19; Red Line Editorial, 22

Press Box Books, an imprint of Press Room Editions.

Library of Congress Control Number: 2020901591

ISBN
978-1-63494-217-1 (library bound)
978-1-63494-235-5 (paperback)
978-1-63494-253-9 (epub)
978-1-63494-271-3 (hosted ebook)

Distributed by North Star Editions, Inc.
2297 Waters Drive
Mendota Heights, MN 55120
www.northstareditions.com

Printed in the United States of America
082020

ABOUT THE AUTHOR

Douglas Lynne is a freelance writer. He spent many years working in the media, first in newspapers and later for online organizations, covering everything from breaking news to politics to entertainment to sports. He lives in Minneapolis, Minnesota.

TABLE OF CONTENTS

IN RARE COMPANY

Devin Booker started off well against the Boston Celtics on March 24, 2017. He led the Phoenix Suns with 10 points in the first quarter. Booker's teammates were used to him leading the way by now. He was averaging more than 20 points per game in just his second season in the National Basketball Association (NBA).

Devin Booker, *left*, drives to the basket during his big game against Boston in 2017.

Booker added eight more points in the second quarter. But the Suns were down by 23 at the half. If Phoenix was to have any chance to win, Booker would have to take over.

Booker heated up in the second half. He was scoring from all over the court. He drove to the hoop for layups. He hit deep three-pointers. He pulled up and made jump shots with defenders in his face. Booker led all scorers with 23 points in the third quarter.

The Celtics players knew he was having a special game. They tried to intimidate him. Boston's Jae Crowder told Booker that he wasn't even going to score 50. Booker already had 41. Fifty was easy.

Booker scored all but one of the Suns' points in the last five minutes of the game. The Celtics could not stop him. They resorted to

Booker lets it fly from long range against the Celtics.

 By the end of the game, even the Boston fans were cheering for Booker to keep scoring.

fouling him in the last minute. Booker scored his final eight points from the free throw line. The final one was his 70th point of the game.

Booker was only 20 years old. That made him the youngest of the six NBA players to score 70 in a game. No one younger had scored even 60 points in a game. Fans could only wonder what he was going to do next.

A SPECIAL ANNIVERSARY

Booker broke the Suns' franchise record for points in a game. The previous record was 60 by Tom Chambers. He accomplished it 27 years earlier, on March 24, 1990.

DEVIN BOOKER, MOST POINTS IN A GAME
THROUGH 2019–20 SEASON

- **70** at Boston, March 24, 2017
- **59** at Utah, March 25, 2019
- **50** vs. Washington, March 27, 2019
- **48** vs. Memphis, March 30, 2019
- **46** at Philadelphia, December 4, 2017

Devin Armani Booker was born on October 30, 1996, in Grand Rapids, a medium-sized city in Western Michigan. He grew up nearby in a suburb called Grandville.

Devin's childhood was different from that of many other kids there. Most people in Grandville were white. Devin's racial background is mixed. His mom, Victoria Gutiérrez, is of Mexican heritage. His dad,

Devin's dad, Melvin Booker (15), was a star guard at Missouri.

Melvin Booker, is black. Devin's parents never married. His dad was often traveling. That's because Melvin was a pro basketball player. He played mostly for minor league teams.

MELVIN BOOKER

Like his son, Melvin Booker was known for his great shooting ability. He became a star at the University of Missouri. But at 6-foot-1, he was considered small, even for a point guard. No NBA team picked him in the 1994 draft. Eventually Melvin played 32 games in the NBA. He spent most of his pro career playing in the US minor leagues and overseas.

Melvin Booker was from Moss Point, Mississippi. Devin often spent summers there. That's where he grew to love basketball. Melvin taught his son proper shooting techniques. Before long, Devin was becoming really good. But he wanted to be great.

So before his sophomore year in high school, Devin moved to Moss Point.

Devin soars for a dunk during Kentucky's season-opening practice.

It was tough at first. The city was very different from Grandville. He thought about moving back to Michigan. Instead, he focused on basketball. Devin spent a lot of time with his dad, who also helped coach his teams. By his senior year, Devin was one of the best players in the country.

Devin had his choice of great college teams to play for. He decided to attend the University of Kentucky. However, several other talented players made the same choice. By then, Devin was a 6'5" guard. He might have been one of the best players in the country. But he didn't start a single game as a freshman.

He didn't need to start to make a big difference on the team, though. Devin had learned to be a smart and unselfish player. He'd developed a great work ethic. He also had a great shot. So when Devin came off the bench, he could make a big impact. His play helped Kentucky reach the 2015 Final Four. After just one college season, he was ready for the NBA.

HERE COMES THE SUN

Devin Booker had made his mark as a sixth man in college. Some believed he needed to prove himself more at Kentucky. The Phoenix Suns saw enough in that one year, though. They picked Booker 13th in the 2015 NBA Draft.

Booker proved the Suns right. After a slow start, he became one of the team's key players. Booker averaged 17.9 points, 3.5 assists, and 3.1 rebounds per game in

Booker poses with his new jersey after the Suns drafted him.

the second half of the season. He also had six 30-point games. At just 19 years old, his future looked bright.

ALL-STAR SHOOTER

The NBA recognized Booker's shooting talent. In 2018, he was invited to take part in the Three-Point Contest during All-Star Weekend. The third-year guard scored 28 points in the final round. That set a new record. He beat Klay Thompson for the title.

After his rookie year, Booker kept getting better. By his second season, he was a full-time starter. He proved to be a big-time scoring threat, too. That was never clearer than in his 70-point game in March 2017 against the Celtics. But Booker scored a lot most nights. His 22.1 points per game in 2016–17 led the Suns. It was the first of many seasons in which that would be the case.

Booker won the Three-Point Contest at the 2018 NBA All-Star Game.

Booker can get to the basket as well as shoot long jumpers.

Most NBA players peak in their mid- to late-20s. Booker got an early start. By his fifth season, in 2019–20, he was a proven scorer. That showed during one hot stretch from

December to January. Booker strung together seven consecutive games with at least 30 points. No Suns player had done that before. Not long after, Booker made his first All-Star Game. He was still just 23 years old.

Booker was more than a scorer. His passing also helped set up his teammates for baskets. The one thing Booker hadn't done after five seasons was lead the Suns to the playoffs. However, after doing so much in his early career, Booker and the Suns looked poised for brighter days ahead.

PHOENIX SUNS CAREER POINTS-PER-GAME LEADERS
THROUGH 2019–20 SEASON

- **Charlie Scott (1972–1975):** 24.8
- **Charles Barkley (1992–1996):** 23.4
- **Devin Booker (2015–):** 22.3

TIMELINE MAP

1. **Grand Rapids, Michigan: 1996**
   Devin Booker is born on October 30.

2. **Chicago, Illinois: 2014**
   Booker scores eight points in 16 minutes on April 2 in the McDonald's All American Game, a showcase for top high school players.

3. **Lexington, Kentucky: 2014–15**
   In his lone season at Kentucky, Booker averages 10.0 points, 2.0 rebounds, and 1.1 assists per game and is named Southeast Conference (SEC) Sixth Man of the Year.

4. **Brooklyn, New York: 2015**
   The Phoenix Suns select Booker with the 13th pick in the NBA Draft on June 25.

5. **Phoenix, Arizona: 2015**
   Booker comes off the bench to score 14 points in his NBA debut on October 28.

6. **Boston, Massachusetts: 2017**
   Booker scores 70 points in a March 24 game against the Celtics.

7. **Phoenix, Arizona: 2018**
   Booker signs a five-year contract extension with the Suns that runs through the 2023–24 season.

8. **Chicago, Illinois: 2020**
   Booker scores six points and grabs four rebounds in his first NBA All-Star Game on February 16.

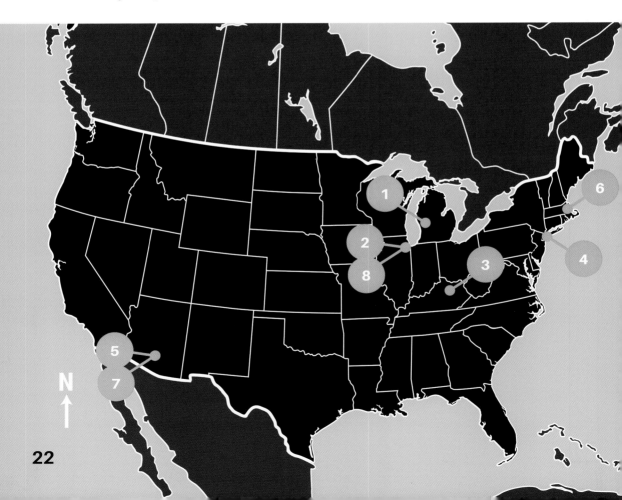

N

AT-A-GLANCE

DEVIN BOOKER

Birth date: October 30, 1996

Birthplace: Grand Rapids, Michigan

Position: Shooting guard

Height: 6 feet 5 inches

Weight: 210 pounds

Current team: Phoenix Suns (2015–)

Past team: Kentucky Wildcats (2014–15)

Major awards: NBA All-Star (2020), NBA All-Rookie First Team (2016), Second Team All-SEC (2015), SEC Sixth Man of the Year (2015), McDonald's All-American (2014)

Accurate through the 2019–20 season.

MORE INFORMATION

To learn more about Devin Booker, go to **pressboxbooks.com/AllAccess**.

These links are routinely monitored and updated to provide the most current information available.

GLOSSARY

draft
A system by which sports leagues divide up new talent.

intimidate
Frighten or threaten someone in order to get them to do what you want.

layup
A shot taken near the basket, often by bouncing the ball off the backboard.

prove
Demonstrate something to be true.

rookie
A first-year player.

sixth man
A basketball player who doesn't start but is usually the first reserve to enter the game.

technique
The proper way to perform a task.

unselfish
Willing to put the needs of others ahead of your own.

INDEX